This book is dedicated to all the amazing friends, family, and people who took the time to encourage and support my writing of this book. Without you, it would have never been possible!

PREFACE

How many times do I hear the same stories: "Scott, I just finished law school and I can't find work, how am I going to pay off my student loans?!" Or, just as often I hear: "Man, I'm working crazy hours at some job that doesn't pay well, and we are so understaffed. I wish I could quit, but it's so hard to find a job these days, I should be more grateful."

Anyone who has spent a considerable amount of time looking for work in the last few years can attest to American songwriter Bob Dylan's famous quote: "The times, they are a changing."

According to the U.S. Bureau of Labor Statistics, the national official unemployment rate was 7.9 % as of January 2013. What most people I've spoken with are unaware of is what statistics are NOT included in this percentage. The unemployment rate we usually hear about is comprised of people actively looking for work and unable to find work within the same month the sample is being conducted. This sample is based on a 4 week period. It does not include:

1) Discouraged workers
2) Persons marginally attached to the labor force
3) Other persons marginally attached to the labor force
4) Total persons employed part time for economic reasons.

Discouraged workers are people who have not looked for work within the past 12 months essentially because they were not able to find work and consequently gave up trying to search for work.

Persons marginally attached to the job market indicate that they currently want and are available for a job and have looked for work sometime in the past 12 months, but have not looked for work within the past 4 weeks.

Other persons marginally attached to the job market want to work but have not looked in the past 4 weeks due to reasons such as ill health, family responsibility, school, transportation issues, and other reasons "not determined."

Persons employed part time for economic reasons are those who want and are available for full-time work but have to settle for a part-time schedule.

If you add up the total number of discouraged workers and other persons marginally attached to the labor force, there are roughly 2,443,000 people NOT COUNTED in the official unemployment rate who currently want to work!

Even more frightening, is that this number DOESN'T even include the people with part time jobs that want to find full time work. In my experience, close to 90 % of the jobs I have been offered within the last year were either part time or temporary jobs. When you factor in "persons employed part-time", there are around 22.7 million (22,748,000) people who currently want to work a full time job in the U.S.

The numbers and percentages strongly speak for themselves. It is my personal belief that a major, if not LARGEST factor that millions of Americans have stopped looking for work, is a result of *frustration by their lack of success throughout the job seeking process.*

In an article published January of 2013, Peter Morici, an economics professor at the University of Maryland, wrote:

"Most of the reduction in unemployment from its 10 percent peak in October 2009 has been accomplished through a significant drop in the percentage of adults working or looking for work. Were the participation rate the same as when President Obama took office, it would be about 10.9 percent."

After having these statistics brought to the reader's attention, I will make a statement: If you do not make a decision to be proactive and put in the work required, much of which is discussed in detail within this book, you will most likely remain in the large percentage of people who are either unemployed, or working a part time job that isn't financially sufficient to their needs. Let's face it, unless you are some rare prodigy or very famous, people aren't going to be banging on your door to offer you work.

The great news: If you make a decision to really work on this area of your life and are willing to make the necessary changes that present themselves, you will have more success in finding work. There are no guarantees in life, and it will take a continuous effort on your part throughout the process. Stay motivated friends!

This being said, the purpose of this book is essentially in response to addressing a vexing, discouraging, and potentially debilitating thing such as not having success with finding work. It's targeted at sharing

1) creative and effective tools providing one with the confidence on knowing what to do during the entire process of finding a job, beginning to end.

2) wisdom, principles and ideas shared from highly successful people throughout our generation.

3) a compilation of personal and interpersonal research, experiences, and theories in an effort to help people throughout this specific process.

Some of the ideas contained in this book may seem unorthodox, or even contrary to popular opinion. Some people also may not agree with everything I have to say, which is quite alright. There was a time when I didn't agree with many of the things I will share with you.

My main objective for writing this book is not to gain the approval of everyone. I wrote this book in an effort to help people get positive results in finding a job, particularly a job that suits their individual gifts and awakens a sense of passion and inspiration within themselves.

"I CAN'T CHANGE THE DIRECTION OF THE WIND, BUT I CAN ADJUST MY SAILS TO ALWAYS REACH MY DESTINATION." Jimmy Dean (American country singer, television host, and creator of the Jimmy Dean Sausage brand)

Being a therapist, I have done my share of reflective listening and counseling in an effort to empower others in different areas of their life. Since the specific subject of job hunting hit so close to home for me, I have had a compelling urge to share my own experiences, successes, and failures with anyone who feels that they would take heed of some helpful ideas and use the extra motivation to go after their dreams. I believe that reading this book will be beneficial in finding work; despite if the present state of the economy is good or bad. My confidence is that a substantial amount of the material in this book will provide the reader (you) with some new ways to approach your job search. Consequently, you will experience a refreshed outlook and motivation.

The ideas and concepts as discussed throughout the book are straightforward, and can be applied by ANYONE. It could be the sixteen year old teenager looking for their first job at the supermarket, the college student who is undecided of a career path, the fifty year old high school teacher who recently got laid off after twenty five years of working, and everyone in between.

A major part of finding work lies in one's ability to establish and develop positive relationships with other people; from the initial contact, email, phone call, interview, etc... In my opinion, the process of "dating" another person shares many similarities with the process of finding work. Dating is a subject anyone can relate to, regardless of what the concept of dating means to them. It offers an additional perspective and reminder of the value of establishing a positive connection with another person. I've found that in addition to the practical insight the comparison makes available to the reader; it can also provide humor and light-heartedness to an otherwise heavy topic.

On a side note, I always welcome feedback. Any success stories in finding work, funny job interview stories, (or not so funny ones,) setbacks, questions, concerns, etc...please, do share! Send an email to thejobinnerviewse@gmail.com. I look forward to hearing from you!

INTRODUCTION

Back in late 2008, I began attending graduate school to be a Marriage and Family Therapist. At the time I currently held a job, and had never had any sort of problems finding work previously. I had hopes, aspirations, and a specialized area of therapy I wanted to work in once graduated. My career goals were looking pretty promising at the time, and I was excited about what potential the future held. Unbeknownst to me, things were about to change..... A LOT. The hours at my job weren't fitting with my school schedule, so I began looking for a job as a waiter in mid - 2009. This seemed to be around the same time that the economy was taking a huge nose dive, off a high dive, and then decided to belly flop for extra effect.

    I had been a waiter for most of college and several years after graduating. I rarely, if ever, had a difficult time finding a restaurant looking for some extra help. I would go to a restaurant during slow hours, meet the manager in person (make a good impression hopefully), and turn in my resume. A formal interview would be set up, and I would get a phone call with a confirmation. If it was a good fit, I was hired. That's pretty straightforward, right?

    I began my hunt now, several years later, and found my experience *drastically different*. I would walk in (during their slow hours), with a big smile on my face, wearing a nice dress shirt, a pair of slacks, and greet the hostess with a handshake with one hand, my resume embraced in the other.

    After my greeting, I would state my purpose and get this type of response. "I'm sorry sir, the manager is busy, and we don't accept applications here. You will need to go fill out an application online, and someone will call you." After following their instructions, weeks would go by with no returned phone calls. I'd call and leave a message. Two more weeks would pass. I would call back asking to speak with a manager and have a conversation such as this one:

Girl at host stand: "Sorry, John (the manager) is in a meeting."

Me: "Well, is there any other manager on staff I can speak with?"

Girl: "No, would you like to leave a message?"

Me: (sigh) "Sure, unless you have a more effective option you wouldn't mind sharing with me."

Girl: "No, that's it."

A lot of the time, I just wanted ANY type of response, even if it was a "no." At least this way I wouldn't feel like I was wasting unnecessary time on one place. Mind you in most cases the establishments I wasn't hearing back from had put ads up online or outside the restaurant stating that they were hiring. Talk about frustrating!

In some places, the staff would actually seem offended and abruptly turned away my resume, saying the same thing: "Go home, fill out an application online. Someone will call you."

Even looking on many career websites and applying online, there seemed to be minimal open positions for anything, and getting a response back from places you applied to was a very one sided relationship.

I contacted former employers, acquaintances, and even friends of mine that were in managerial positions. Almost EVERY ONE of them said something to this effect: "Scott, I would love to hire you, (again) but unfortunately I recently had to fire current staff because we can't afford to keep them on payroll. A lot of these people worked for me over the last 5 years and were great employees. I'm really sorry."

Sound all too familiar? If you can relate to feeling this way, than I hope you keep reading, because *it doesn't have to be this way.*

I spent the good part of 3 years looking for jobs, and I put in a lot of work to find work! (Who would have thought?) Like most things, if you practice and practice at it, you start to get a little bit better, certain things become a little more natural, and you hopefully learn from mistakes. Along with myself, there are many job seekers I talk to that have had to accept the new challenges of looking for work and adapt to the situation at hand.

There are things that I have learned along the way: networking tips, the dos, the don'ts, when to call, what to say, and pre-interview, interview, and post interview etiquette I picked up as a direct result of all my job searching.

For instance, with our increasingly rapid acceleration of technology, how is a job seeker nowadays supposed to instinctively know that they need to convert their attached resume in an email to a PDF file, just in case the recipient's computer doesn't properly accept a Microsoft Word document? Or, at what point did it become almost standard procedure to send a follow up email after an interview thanking the person who conducted the interview?

I know I was certainly unaware of these things, as are numerous job seekers I have spoken with.

The question then becomes such: Where on earth is there a guide book that can inform us of these things, and other useful tips, so we don't unknowingly shoot ourselves in the foot while trying to land a job?

Well, that is precisely why I decided to write this book. My hope is that the content within this book can be a guide and compass to you as you set out and embark on this seemingly perilous voyage. I have spoken with many well established people that are up to date and successful in the present economy, and interviewed people that have been in positions of hiring; ranging anywhere from five years of hiring experience to thirty years of experience. Additionally I have done a great deal of research on the subject in both a literary and tangible sense of the word. Throughout the process of writing this book I also interviewed people who were able to land jobs in the given economy and how they were able to find success and overcome different obstacles despite having setbacks along the way. My goal has been to concisely pack in as many useful tips and tools for the reader to have at their fingertips and grab hold of.

Use this guide as you see fit along your journey.

CHAPTER 1: A FRESH PERSPECTIVE

"GOOD JUDGEMENT COMES FROM EXPERIENCE, EXPERIENCE COMES FROM BAD JUDGEMENT"
~Jim Horning (notable computer scientist, founder of STAR Lab)

DON'T TAKE IT PERSONAL:

I will add that to my own experience, the type of treatment I received from establishments (managers, administration, etc.) has been equally, if not more discouraging, than the scarcity of jobs available. Repeatedly being turned down from work through an email, a phone call never returned about a job, and feeling brushed aside by employers over time left me with a gnawing feeling of rejection and inadequacy. Deep down I believed and reminded myself that I was a good worker, had many gifts to offer, and recalled positive feedback from previous employers. However, as the pattern of not being able to find work persisted, these feelings would eventually dissipate and be replaced by resentment and frustration. Even when I mustered the energy to be positive and upbeat over the phone with a manager or administrator, a lot of the time I just felt as though they were very short with me and bothered by my attempting to look for work. I will expand and elaborate more on this matter shortly.

THE MINDSET:

The search for a job and dating share many similarities. In both instances, there is generally a process of getting contact info (digits), developing an initial rapport, and setting up the first encounter.

I began to realize over time that employers nowadays have so many options of great potential candidates, consistently and desperately asking to be hired, many have developed a certain type of attitude. It is an attitude such that, hot celebrities like Brad Pitt or Beyonce might have towards their thousands upon thousands of admirers that would do anything to go on date with them. My observation of our present job market, for all intents and purposes, is this: **Most Employers have developed a similar mindset to that of an "A" list celebrity.**

Sound like a bold or extreme analogy? Well, that was the point. Think about this for a moment: if you were Brad Pitt or Beyonce, and had dozens, hundreds, sometimes thousands of people contacting you to go on a date on a daily basis, can you imagine how picky and selective you would need to become just for your mere sanity!

On a similar note: *Have you ever thought for a moment and put yourself in the EMPLOYER'S SHOES?* I have, and it makes a HUGE difference in my interactions with potential employers. Over the years, I have spent a good amount of time observing, asking questions, and listening to employers to have a greater understanding of this. They are generally understaffed (usually due to the economy), and still need to get their daily job duties done in addition to hearing from all these people looking for work. Tall order, no? I have friends on the opposite end (employers) and they can attest to this. Anyone, given the right set of circumstances, could begin to develop the mindset I mentioned above.

The statement above was not meant to portray an employer as 'bad' in any sense, but rather to get the reader (you) to think about the situation differently. Remember when I mentioned earlier how I was feeling 'resentful and frustrated' with employers? Well, it took a combination of a deeper understanding and acceptance to begin to have a shift in my perception. This was/is not always easy for me to maintain; it takes work and dedication. If you can develop this awareness as you are applying for work, I believe you will be at a strong advantage.

This being said, what do we (job searchers) need to do to stand out from the thousands of others? Well, let's return to dating for a moment. What kind of person would stand out in an "A - list celebrities "mind from all their 'other suitors'? Being realistic; there are thousands (perhaps millions) of beautiful, talented men and women around the world that would love to be with Brad Pitt or Beyonce. What might a few qualities be that these individuals can possess to separate themselves from the rest?

How about specializing in something that others don't, and being able to offer this something to the other person in a way that suits their needs and/or desires?

Having different and interesting attributes that are attractive to the other person you're connecting with.

Demonstrating value and confidence when establishing a connection with a new person you meet.

These are just a few examples. The point is here that if you have a uniquely attractive talent, gift, or quality that others don't, it will be intriguing and potentially valued in both dating and job hunting. The **Law of Differentiation** states that the less you differentiate yourself from others, the more price sensitive people become. On the other hand, the more you differentiate yourself, the less price sensitive people become. A present-day example of this would be how many consumers have been willing to spend a lot more money on an iPhone over its competitors simply because of the way the product differentiated itself. I personally believe that if you begin to fully grasp this law and continuously search for new ways to apply it, you will inevitably increase your success rate exponentially.

PREDICT THE FUTURE:

If you are deciding on a career path for the first time, or a change in careers, I highly recommend that you do your homework and look at some of today's leading industries, especially what industries have a high projected growth in the FUTURE.

NHL hall of famer and all-time leading scorer Wayne Gretzky said, "I skate to where the puck is going to be, not to where it has been."

Looking backward within the last decade or so, a lot of people realized the huge need for an RN (Registered Nurse) in our job market. Many people took advantage of this situation and were able to find work. Some years later, going to school to become a Registered Nurse is highly competitive and heavily impacted, and people I know aren't finding work as nurses without difficulty. On the other hand, those people who had the foresight to see this industry growing 15 years ago had a much easier time finding work and getting into nursing schools.

An example in our present job market of 'skating to where the puck is going to be' is a newer degree offered, a 'Computer Security Degree.' This is a degree which trains students to protect computers from viruses, digital threats, and spam emails. It should be obvious as to why this is a very necessary skill in our economy, and since this particular degree is so new, there will be more of a need for people graduating with a computer security degree. If this is something you have a passion for and are skilled at, I recommend looking into it.

Other things you can do in the research of top growing industries would be

> 1) Reading the business section of a reputable newspaper or magazine (Wall Street Journal, New York Times, Los Angeles Times, Newsweek, Forbes, etc.)

2) Paying close attention to social media (what's trendy, things the majority are currently buying or interested in)

3) Connecting with people who are well established in their career and up to date on current market trends.

On another note, maybe the type of work you love doing isn't a rapidly growing industry. Great, at least you've done some soul searching and realized what you want to do. Still, it wouldn't hurt to dedicate some extra time and look into what industries are expanding, and which ones are struggling. For example, the field I received my Master's degree in is much more heavily impacted than it was ten years ago. There are a significantly higher number of people graduating with this degree, and if that wasn't bad enough; also less jobs available. What a terrific combination!

Joking aside, this isn't to say that the field isn't going to expand in the future with more job opportunities. The reason I share this example is because if I had chosen another career path that was growing and still allowed me to utilize my gifts and interests, I might have not had as big of a struggle to find work upon graduating.

In any event, the idea here is that by doing your homework beforehand, you may come up with effective ways to pick a field you want to be in and be successful as well.

Assuming by now I have assessed my strengths, picked a career path, and found ways to contribute my gifts, another obstacle then presents itself: How do I even get ahold of this person to show them just how 'special and interesting' I am?

NETWORKING:
I personally had to get honest with myself about this over the past several years. As much as I hated to admit it, being qualified

(many times overqualified), hard-working, professional, personable, creative, etc. was still not getting me jobs. Once in a while, I would hear back from employers, sometimes even get an interview. However, for every 50 applications I would fill out, I may get one or two potential interviews. Those interviews either didn't land me the job, or were probably my last choice for a place to work.

On the other hand, the girl who has a friend working camera man on the set of a film starring Mr. Pitt will most likely have much "easier access" in getting an opportunity to meet her dream man than most the competition, solely because of who she knows. It simply is what it is.

TIMING:

Note that the girl's friend mentioned above was 'currently' working on the Brad Pitt movie, so her timing was right. Had it been a year, or even six months earlier, her friend could possibly be working on a different film and may not have had contact with Brad Pitt.

There have been many occasions where I knew the right people, but my 'timing' wasn't in line. On the other hand, I have also experienced the combination of both, and gotten a job as a result. The important thing to remember is that just because the timing may not be 'right' at one point, it *doesn't mean it won't be perfect timing eventually.*

I cannot stress this fact enough, so hopefully the italics helped for reinforcement! It will prove helpful to make a list of your best networks and contacts. Remain in good standing with them, and try to help these people in their endeavors whenever it is in your ability to do so. If something is meant to be, an opportunity will blossom in its due season, and you may be the one who reaps the rewards. At the very least you have begun to condition yourself in establishing and maintaining positive relationships with regards to your network, and have hopefully helped some people along the way.

IT IS ABOUT WHO YOU KNOW:

I have personally found that currently (2012-2013) LinkedIn is a GREAT networking tool. As a matter of fact, I landed a job over a year ago by going onto one of my groups and stating, "I recently moved to the area, and I'm looking for work. I specialize in X,Y,and Z. Does anyone have any suggestions?" Not only did I get some references, but I had someone email me offering me a job! Nice! Signing up on LinkedIn is simple: (www.linkedin.com). A basic account is entirely free, and will provide you with great resource and network opportunities.

In his book *Little black book of Networking,* Jeffrey Gitomer speaks about seeing how you can first add value or help people you would network with. I was actually able to get a few interviews simply by emailing random people in my area and sharing my expressed interests that I noticed on their website. If you come in with a positive, helpful frame of mind and are willing to walk away if nothing comes of it, you will be surprised at things that can come to fruition.

I have personally found the potential for positive impact by expanding one's network now more than ever before. And if you don't know many influential people, get to know them! Who knows, maybe Brad Pitt's cameraman is on LinkedIn!

Having names, connections, and a good rapport has been VERY effective in my job hunt, especially when done before even applying anywhere!

EXPANDING YOUR NETWORK:

I have learned over time that even getting turned down from a job could be an opportunity to network. Whenever I discovered I wasn't hired for the position I interviewed for, I would do a few simple things. One was, I would thank them, and tell them I was very determined and passionate to do what I love for work. Next, I posed the question of what the person thought I could do to improve my chances of getting work in my field. Towards the end of the conversation, I would then ask them if they knew any other people I could contact that may be hiring.

More often than not, people hearing this (assuming they had a heart, and were also somewhat passionate about their work), were more than happy to share what they could. Not only that, but if they already met me in person and liked me, I usually had no problem getting the employer to agree to give me a recommendation if contacted. Now, I not only had more leads, but a REFERALL! So I would then call these places, and state: "Jane Smith over at (insert company name) referred me to your company, and she mentioned you guys needed someone for this position, etc." ..... See where I am going with this ?

VOLUNTEERING:

This is obviously a positive thing to do in any type of setting where you can be of service. Volunteering is a great way to make connections with others, and you just never know who you might meet along the way. The people on committees or working a charity event are typically kind hearted and helpful individuals. I mean why else would you "volunteer" your time working without making money to serve the community?

The ideal situation would be to volunteer for a local committee or organization that connects in some way to the type of work you would like to be doing. When I was living in San Diego, I offered to help out an Autism Advocacy group hosting a "back to school" meeting for parents of children with Autism. The people running it seemed very friendly, and I asked them what I could do to help. I suggested being a greeter, bringing pastries, cleaning up, whatever was needed.

The group leader had another idea, and asked me to give a speech to the parents in attendance. The subject was for me to discuss different calming techniques for their kids to use (and themselves perhaps) while adjusting to beginning a new school year. It caught me off guard a bit, especially getting the call 2 days prior, but I told them it would be an honor. The speech went really well, and I met some amazing parents, special education attorneys, and teachers that work within the Autistic community. I still remain in contact with some of these people to this very day.

A good friend of mine shared this same idea of the importance of volunteering. He is very bright and has a PhD in International Relations, yet couldn't find any work. Just recently he decided to volunteer for a local campaign in our community. Within a few months, he went from volunteering a few days a week, to being hired on within this campaign full time. I know he is thoroughly enjoying the work he is doing right now, and is getting some excellent experience working alongside some very talented people.

Some of you may be thinking, "Sure, I'd love to volunteer, but I can't afford to volunteer full time and support myself!" Of course, this is perfectly understandable! Not everyone is in a position to be able to volunteer full time, and the former paragraph was just an example. However, there is no reason why you can't at least volunteer for an event that is held once a year, or perhaps with some type of committee that meets on a monthly basis. Start with something small if it suits you best, and take it from there.

Volunteering feels good, provides a sense of contribution, and can be particularly uplifting to a person's spirit while searching for work. Not to mention that in my experience, the universe seems to have a funny way of taking care of you when you offer to help others. In particular, this holds true when you are sincerely doing the best you can to help without having any sort of expectations of "what's in it for me?"

There are tons of ways to volunteer. A few examples would be working a fundraising event such as a Walk for Crone's disease or an AIDS marathon. In relation to your career interests, Google search the types of companies you are interested in and I guarantee you that on many company websites or blogs you will see ways to get involved. Personally, I've found that joining different groups on Meetup.com and LinkedIn to be very useful. On the Meetup website you can search the types of things you are interested in, and it will provide you with many groups in your local area. Even if you can't find something related to your work, why not go to a weekly gathering with something you love, like softball or volleyball? If you make yourself available, undoubtedly opportunities to contribute will present themselves.

ASK QUESTIONS:

If you have friends or family members that do interviews and hiring, I STRONGLY encourage you to ask them about what things make or break a potential job opportunity. If you don't have family in these types of positions, contact one! It could be as simple as someone you're connected with through a friend on LinkedIn. Write them an email stating: "Hey, I noticed that you were friends with 'so and so' as well. I have been looking for work and have not had much success, and I was wondering if you could give me any advice on the interview process that might be useful to know. " There are so many things I would have never known beforehand if I hadn't asked these sorts of questions myself.

Carl Jung, a world renowned author and psychotherapist, had this to say: "To ask the right question is already half the solution to the problem." Additionally, different employers look for different things. So the point to remember, just like with dating, is that some things are SUBJECTIVE. You may not be a good fit for one company, but that certainly does not mean that you won't be 'just the right person for the job' with another company. Similarly, one guy may want to date an outgoing, boisterous, and athletic girl, while another guy may be looking for a more intellectual, artistic, and introverted girl.

Regardless of personal taste, I do strongly believe is that if you develop a good rapport, show a positive attitude, and exude a respectable level of self-assurance, you are off to a great start. This holds true on both a job interview and a date.

KEY POINTS TO REMEMBER FROM CHAPTER 1:

- Do not to take it personally when you don't receive responses from potential employers for a while. This is what the majority of people experience in our economy. Do learn to always look where you could have improved to make a connection work in the future.

- Understanding and developing an awareness of the employer and the added challenges they face can enable you to accept the current situation better and find creative ways to find solutions to problems.

- Brainstorm with yourself and others about what skills, certifications, experiences, etc. can separate you from others in your particular field. Make a list of these and continue to add to it as you search for work. The Law of Differentiation is a powerful law when used properly.

- Figure out or expand on your current career path. The ability to research your industry and its growth/decline can prevent making unnecessary mistakes if you can adapt and see opportunities.

- Find out the fastest growing industries and envision what industries will continue to grow in the future. Read business related newspapers/magazines, pay attention to social media, and speak with others who are highly successful and up to date on current trends in the market.

- Networking and timing are essential and one of the most effective tools to use in finding work. Build your network and learn as much as you can about how to grow in this area. Volunteering in your local community, social networking, connecting with friends, family, old classmates, and former employers/colleagues are all great methods of expanding your network.

CHAPTER 2: PRESENT YOURSELF POSITIVELY FROM THE START

When you have a direction (or multiple ones) picked, there are certainly things one should do before they even begin to hop on their iPad/laptop/I-phone/notebook/desktop and search for job openings. Think of preparing for a first date, what do you do? It's a little different for everyone I'm sure, but let's play a round of Family Feud and generalize, shall we?

- Buying new clothes
- Washing your car
- Getting a haircut
- Putting on your favorite fragrance
- Grooming (shower, shaving, mani/pedi, plucking evil stray hairs, etc)
- Picking a good location to go to.

One trait ALL these answers seem to have in common is this: A conscious effort on your part to make the best first impression that you can.

This being said, shouldn't we put in just as much, if not more, time, money, and effort into making the best possible impression on future employers? I hope you answered yes. If not, maybe your goal is to be a trophy husband or wife, in which event I'm not sure why you would be wasting time reading this book!

GETTING STARTED:

For all the rest of you desiring to find a great job, let's begin with a resume. In creating a resume, it is always helpful to go on websites with templates of effective resumes to use as a guide. There are many job search sites that provide easy to follow instructions on making a resume.

I asked several employers what are important things that make ones resume stand out. First, your resume should be specifically geared towards the type of job you want to apply for. I had about 3 different resumes saved on my computer at one point: One towards counseling/mental health, another towards sales/marketing, and the third service industry. This is extremely useful, with the exception being if you have only had two or three jobs before the current one you're applying for. In any case, the resume should highlight one's best qualifications, skills, and experience in relation to the specific job you are applying for. Many times, this will change from interview to interview, so I highly recommend making the necessary changes you need to on a case by case basis.

COVER LETTER:

In my experience, while not every company requires you to provide a cover letter, it is still imperative to know how to write a great cover letter. As a matter of fact, one pattern I noted when interviewing people who successfully found work, was that they would almost always attach a cover letter when applying for a job, even if it wasn't requested on the application or by the employer. The cover letter is, essentially, your chance to summarize why you would be an ideal candidate for the job that you are applying for. Be as detailed and specific as you can about how your qualifications and experience would make you a good fit for the particular position. What you write will most likely vary a bit with different positions. You wouldn't list the exact same individual qualifications and aspirations in applying for a job as a financial consultant as you would a bartender, would you?

From the employers I have spoken with, it is ideal to be concise and to the point with a cover letter as well. Having a heading, "I'm applying for the position of (blank)" with two or three well written paragraphs should suffice. To save you the exhaustion and frustration of having to write a cover letter from scratch every time, I recommend having a few generalized cover letters you wrote saved on a computer or flash drive. This way in the event the position you are applying for is similar to a job you previously applied to, you can upload the saved document and customize it to fit the current position.

REFERENCES:

If you have had some experience in the work history department, most likely you have had a few potential employers ask you to provide references for them to contact your previous employers. And most likely, you know that if they call/email to ask you to provide references at some point after your interview, it is usually a final step before deciding to offer you a position. This being said, it behooves you to have the best references possible!

From my experience, it is ideal to have at least 5 great references. Employers I have worked for in the past wanted to speak with three of my former employers before being hired. This being said, it is well worth the time to make sure the top 3 references you give are people that you know are reliable and will return phone calls and emails! I certainly learned over the years that although some of my previous employers were great people that I had strong relationships with, they were not the greatest at their response time. Believe me when I tell you that if you're in the final phase where references are being checked, you want the people who you know are the most efficient in responding and will say positive things about you.

One obstacle in this situation is that you can never be certain that previous employers will say fantastic things about you. What I have usually done is used my better judgment and contacted the people I felt I had the strongest relationships with and were genuinely interested in my success. I let them know that I'm looking for work and that I was going to use them as a reference. Considering the present circumstances, (amount of time that has passed since working for them, # of employees they have working for them, etc.) I may remind them of what positive feedback they gave me during my employment with them.

Towards the end of the conversation, I will generally say something to the effect of: "I greatly appreciate you returning my call/email, as I realize how busy you are. In the future, would it be more convenient for you to be reached by email or phone by these employers?" This question has been fail proof for me, and they usually seem pleased that I was being considerate of their time. Not only that, but I've also noticed that the effort I made in contacting them resulted in them responding very promptly down the road with potential employers!

Presently, I am fortunate enough to know which of my references say very positive things about me, mainly because the people who hired me over the years told me directly (as I was meeting to sign paperwork): "Scott, Elizabeth Smith and John Lemons had such great things to say about you!" The point is that if you make an extra effort to create a list of strong references and contact them, it will pay off when you need it most!

PERSONAL APPEARANCE:
Being well-groomed, dressing appropriately, and basic hygiene are essential. My hope is that the benefit of a professional appearance is already obvious to the reader. If not, I hope it becomes obvious really soon, or you're in trouble! In either a potential job situation or speaking with a new girl I've just met, I typically feel much more confident when I'm well groomed, dressed nicely, etc.

In my opinion, the way you dress for an interview in the professional world should be one of the few things you do that DOESN'T cause you stand out from other job candidates. Of course, there are many exceptions to this rule. Perhaps if you're looking for work in the fashion industry this need not apply, in which case I would suggest consulting with others in that industry about the "do's and don'ts" in regards to how to dress for an interview.

For the majority of us, the consensus is to err on the side of being conservative.

MEN: having some nice dress shirts, slacks, and ties readily available is a plus. Make sure you take good care of your clothes, including ironing or pressing, with no visible holes, tags, or pins still left on from the dry cleaners. Even if you don't have much money to spend, you can find some good deals shopping online, or even a Nordstrom Rack, Macy's, TJ Maxx, etc...While your clothes don't have to be brand new fore say, definitely avoid wearing clothes that are faded, have stains, or torn in half. You get the idea........

WOMEN: skirts at the mid- thigh and below range are acceptable, so it would probably be better to save the daisy dukes and apple bottom jeans for another occasion. A girlfriend of mine told me that a common mistake girls make are wearing shoes that have open toes and closed toe shoes are appropriate dress code for an interview.

In regards to tattoos and facial piercings, it is best to not have either exposed to the person interviewing you. Again, there are exceptions to the rule, such as applying for a job as a tattoo artist or to be on a reality TV show. These types of positions may very likely favor the display of tattoos and piercings.

As for cologne/perfumes, a word to the wise and avoid overdoing it. You probably enjoy your fragrance, but the person interviewing you may not feel the same way. Additionally, they might even be allergic to a certain perfume or cologne. If I do wear cologne, I use it very sparingly and apply it at least a few hours before my interview begins.

I believe your personal appearance and attire is more about AVOIDING making a negative first impression during the interview than trying to CREATE a positive impression. Again, using good judgment and doing your homework on the "do's and don'ts" in this area would be wise. Don't worry; you'll have plenty of time to stand out in other positive ways during your conversations throughout the interview.

MORE ON PRESENTATION:

In Lou Adler's "*The essential guide for hiring and getting hired,* " he stated: "Most interviewers unconsciously react to the candidate's first impression, good and bad. If bad, they become uptight, convinced the person is not qualified. The unconscious bias causes them to ask tougher questions, going out of their way to prove the candidate is not qualified. They minimize the positive and maximize the negatives. Sometime during the interview the bias dissipates, but for those candidates that start out in the doghouse it's often too late, with the person never being seriously considered or evaluated. "

"In comparison, prospects who are prepared, confident, friendly, outgoing, communicative, and professional in appearance tend to be instantly considered viable candidates for the open position, even if they lack basic skills. Under the influence of a positive first impression interviewers relax, become more open minded, tend to ask easier questions, maximizing the positives and minimizing the negatives. Their unconscious objective is to prove the candidate is qualified."

KEY POINTS TO REMEMBER FROM CHAPTER 2:

- Positive presentation is essential in making a first impression and can make or break job opportunities. Use different tools and speak with employers about how to make the best impact possible with your resume, cover letter, references, etc.

- Create a few Cover Letters to have ready to send to inquiring employers. Make a list and get in touch with at least three of your strongest references. Find out the most effective way they can be reached so when the time comes your future employer will be able to contact them.

- Put in the extra effort to look your best in an interview (clothes, haircut, shoes). While you're personal grooming and clothes may not be the deciding factor in getting hired, it can certainly hurt your chances if you show up and give off an unprofessional appearance before you even open your mouth to speak.

CHAPTER 3: "APPLY"ING YOURSELF

Let's state the obvious and not sugarcoat this: APPLYING FOR JOBS IS NOT FUN! Repeat it with me this time, and say it like you mean it.....
    APPLYING FOR JOBS IS NOT FUN!!!!! Ok, feel better? I know I do.
    The search for work can be very tedious, time consuming, and frustrating! Knowing this, it's no wonder people (myself included) resist this activity like the Bubonic plague. I feel like a major reason why people nowadays stay at jobs they hate, is because they remember how freaking awful it is to apply for work! Or, there is the person that gets comfortable being able to sleep in and collect their unemployment, and don't have that sense of urgency bothering them to find work. I'm not implying that there is anything wrong with this, as there are about a million more interesting things I can find to do aside from looking for work myself. The only setback I've seen happen repeatedly is getting too at ease with not working and then waiting to start applying at the last minute when the unemployment checks stop coming in. I usually suggest people set realistic goals for themselves when it comes to applying places. It is additionally helpful to anticipate the setbacks and to not get down on oneself for resisting looking for work. I have yet to meet a person that hasn't experienced this resistance, especially when the job hunt lasts for an extended length of time. It's part of the journey, a necessary evil.

EFFECTIVE TIME MANAGEMENT:
    Highly successful entrepreneur and New York Times bestseller Timothy Ferris, supports a particular theory in his book: 4 *HOUR*

WORK WEEK. As the title of the book implies, Ferris suggests learning how to become more successful in a career while working less. One idea that he expanded on throughout the book was: "If you give yourself a time constraint to accomplish something, you will be much more productive."

I have personally found that setting a goal of applying for jobs for an hour a day is a lot less overwhelming than thinking, "Oh my god, I need a job and I'm going to spend 10 hours tomorrow looking for work." Now don't get me wrong, part of looking for work can be a simple numbers game.

If you feel like applying with twenty-five to a hundred different establishments a day is what you need to do, go right ahead.

I have had that mentality at a point and implemented it, only to get burnt out REALLY fast with minimal results. Plus, there was always an incredible amount of procrastination involved, so I'd be lucky to have put in an actual 2-3 hours looking for work even if I had intended it to be 5-8 hours.

A trick I used that helped me to work more efficiently: Whenever I knew I would be doing most of my job hunt on a laptop for that particular day, I would go anywhere aside from my home (coffee shop, library) and purposely NOT bring my laptop charger. This way, I knew I would only have several hours to work on my laptop before the power ran out, which was very effective at preventing me from finding anyone or anything to distract my attention away from actually doing the painstaking task at hand.
*** Note: (This was something that worked for me, simply because I personally tend to get distracted REALLY easily, ESPECIALLY when it comes to job hunting!)

The key is to know yourself, and how YOU perform work and complete tasks, this way you can set yourself up for success. If you know someone else currently looking for work, you can go to a coffee shop, internet café, etc. and job hunt together. Use one another as accountability partners, (similar to workout partners) in an effort to stay on track. These are just a few ideas; choose the things that work best for you.

SEARCHING FOR WORK ON THE WEB

In addition to the specific sites I have geared towards my field, I have found sites like Craig's list, Simply Hired, Glassdoor, CareerBuilder, and LinkedIn to be very useful. Also, if you go on your local county website, they will usually have a list of approved sites to go on to look for work.

The method I have found that works best for me is to create some variation: An example would look something like this:

Monday: Call my current networks and inquire about different opportunities.

Tuesday: LinkedIn, Craig's List

Wednesday: CareerBuilder, SimplyHired, Glassdoor

Thursday: Prepare for 2 interviews

Friday: 9am Interview, 2pm Interview.

Saturday: Relax!

Sunday: Optional/additional work related sites.

I've also found it very helpful to keep a list of the companies I've applied for and a few basic facts about them (type of position, name of hiring manager, name of person emailed, phone number, etc.). It kept me organized, and I would write the jobs I wanted the most at the top of the list, along with the date I applied there. Since so often it takes months and months to hear back from places, being organized and having the information at hand can keep you on track and more focused.

GENERATION EMAIL:

When applying for work, keep in mind that it is ALWAYS a good idea to remind people you're emailing (if you were referred) of *the person who referred you*. The recipients are extremely busy, and uhh, human too. They don't always remember everything that your friend at J.P. Morgan told them on their 5 minute coffee break during a 10 hour workday. I've also found if the situation warrants, emailing two contacts you already spoke with in one email can be a great way to get a response. Not only does this separate you from the thousand other people looking for work, but I personally believe that people are often motivated by saving face, and if done properly and in a graceful manner, you will sometimes get prompt responses from both people you sent the application to.

Keep in mind that this method isn't always conducive or necessary. In the instances I do decide to use this method, I usually will address both people I am emailing in the content of the email and explain its intended purpose. Otherwise, this technique can come off as invasive or confusing to the recipients.

While on the current topic of emailing, I would like to address something that is often overlooked, but can certainly be a deal breaker with employers. *Make sure that the emails you send out in your job search use proper grammar, correct spelling, and are well written*! Text messaging has rapidly become the most widely used form of communication in America. "Texting," depending on the person, can entail a large amount of informal conversation (Think "lol," "brb," and "ttyl"). I have heard from many people that are ASTOUNDED at the content of emails that they receive from job applicants nowadays. This occurrence seems to be more prevalent of the younger generation from what I hear. Whatever the case may be, don't fall into this category! I would suggest always proofreading before sending out an email. While you're at it, maybe ask yourself these types of questions:

- Does my email communicate my point clearly?
- Did it answer specific questions needed by the employer?
- What would I think of the job candidate if I was an employer reading this email?

If possible, have some people you know in the professional world take a look over the content of the emails you typically send out to employers.

Personally, I have experimented with the formal/informal nature of my email. The reason I did this is to begin with was based on my knowledge of the volume of emails the employer will generally get on a daily basis. To clarify, I wasn't saying "Wussup man?" or "Check my resume out bro, it's awesome!"

I WAS, however, experimenting with a more general level of being personable: (acting like we had known each other for a while, expressing a little more enthusiasm about the job opportunity, etc.) I did this in hopes of standing out *just a little bit* from the other five hundred people that sent out emails and resumes that day.

This kind of communication was done on a case by case basis for me. I do not have any statistical analysis one way or the other on its effect. However, my experience has been that if the recipient responds back (especially in a personable way), that a good rapport is developed much more quickly.

In any event, the former paragraph was intended to give the reader (you) another point to consider when you're sending out dozens of emails attached with your resume daily. While it might not be wise to go overboard on this concept, I don't see the harm in trying to experiment yourself. Worst case scenario, they don't respond back, which happens 90% of the time anyways! At the very least it can lessen the mundane and boring nature of sending email after email to employers. Maybe the person who gets five hundred emails per day was just thinking how tedious it is to read all those emails and welcomed something a bit more upbeat and creative. Just a thought.

KEY POINTS TO REMEMBER FROM CHAPTER 3:

- Finding work can be a very tedious and painstaking journey. Anticipating resistance or setbacks and setting realistic individual goals will be very useful throughout the process.

- Learn to effectively manage your time looking for work and create variety and structure whenever possible. Prioritizing will improve organization, increase productivity, and prevent "burnout".

- Continue to improve your skills in sending out emails. Content, grammar, punctuation, etc. are all things in your control and can make a lasting impression for better or worse.

- Find ways to build a positive rapport with employers from the very beginning. It will help you standout and produce significant results if done correctly.

Hopefully, at this point you will start getting some replies, which leads us to:

CHAPTER 4: GETTING READY FOR THE FIRST DATE

Does anyone remember the movie *Van Wilder?* The 'Animal House' style comedy was about a seven year veteran college student named Van, who made a college career of partying. Van Wilder was played by actor Ryan Reynolds. It's quite an entertaining movie.

There was a scene in the movie when Reynolds character meets a beautiful school reporter Gwen, (Tara Reid) whose editor wants her to do an interview with him for the school paper. Reynolds begins to flirt with Reid's character while confirming a time to meet to conduct the interview, saying "It's a date." When Reid quickly corrects him; he objects and replies back, "Gwen, first dates are interviews."

While there certainly seems to be some truth to that statement, I believe the concept, *"First interviews are dates"* can apply as well. This doesn't include the potential for the physical component (c'mon now folks!) I am, however, suggesting that the initial encounter with your potential employer is to establish some type of chemistry, a good connection, and the possible agreement of wanting to see the other person again.

Having an upcoming interview is one of my favorite parts of the process, (except for the whole getting hired thing) because

A) You're already getting that first interview (or date)

B) It gives you the chance to meet someone in person, assuming it's not a phone interview, which is still more personable than an email.

C) You can now have time to be more creative, assertive, and intriguing; having a greater chance in improving your odds of getting hired (versus applications that often don't get looked at, or take months to hear back about)

KNOW YOUR AUDIENCE:

What do I mean by this? Well, as some may already know and do, it is very important to research the company/person that you plan to interview for. Not only will this provide you with how you can contribute to the business, but it will help you come up with good questions, and give you an opportunity to *qualify the interviewer.*

One thing I more recently learned was from reading Dale Carnegie's *HOW TO WIN FRIENDS AND INFLUENCE PEOPLE.* * There is a chapter in the book where he describes how Theodore Roosevelt was able to get along with anyone. A tool that he used was that before meeting with anyone, he spent time researching the individual and finding out what their passions, hobbies, and interests were.

> *'How to win friends and influence people' was one of the first best-selling self-help books of its time, and it to date is still at the top of the list. Published in 1936, it has sold over 15 million copies to date.

According to Carnegie, it didn't matter if Roosevelt had any interest in those particular subjects either. Rather, it was the *genuine interest in the other person.* "The royal road to a person's heart; is to talk about the thing that person treasures most."

With all the qualified candidates out there, don't you think a person will be more likely to hire you if you go for a spin on this "royal road," develop a good rapport, and they like you?

I think so as well.

I remember a specific instance when, before interviewing, I researched the individual and noticed that she had an interest for Kundalini Yoga. Having a similar interest myself, I mentioned it at the beginning of the interview.

The first thirty minutes of the interview became a conversation about yoga and its benefits and also dialogue about traveling. As she became excited, she began to open up to me about some of her other passions. Paradoxically, I was the person who eventually began to transition the conversation back into discussing the job description. Can you imagine how much more fluid and enjoyable the rest of the interview went than if I hadn't developed that rapport in the beginning?!

It seemed to also be much more enjoyable for the person interviewing me, which obviously goes a long way when it comes time for them to decide who to hire. Oddly enough, or 'remarkably enough,' the person who I mentioned above *contacted me* as I was going through my final editing phase for this book. I had sent out an email to a lot of people inquiring about different titles for this book and what they liked best. It turns out her email was on that list of people. She contacted me, gave me some feedback, and said "Wow, Scott, you're always doing something interesting, this is exciting!" Keep in mind, this is a woman I met ONE TIME IN MY LIFE for an interview, and she had no clue that I referenced her in my story. For all the people she sees on a daily basis, I must have made a good impression, right? Case in point!

MORE ON ESTABLISHING RAPPORT:

I'll give you another example. I specifically remember making plans to hang out with a very attractive girl I had just recently met. After adding her as a friend on Facebook, I noticed she had recently posted pictures of a trip she took to Costa Rica. I was fortunate enough to have visited that country and had a great experience in my travels. Consequently, I then had a commonality with this girl that not everyone else in Southern California may have had with her, or if they did, it might not be something they would randomly bring up when first introducing themselves.

On a side note, and after speaking with many women on the subject, many a beautiful girl will attest to guys trying very hard to impress them in the initial stages of meeting, and at some point in this initial stage will tell them how beautiful they are. For the record, I don't see anything "wrong" with telling a girl she is beautiful. I certainly have done so to every woman I've ever had a long term relationship with, and some in between. The point is, based on feedback I've gotten from these women; guys seem to want to tell them right off the bat: "Wow, you are just so incredibly beautiful."

Based on what I've gathered, this seems to be a reoccurring theme throughout most attractive women's lives. The words themselves are undoubtedly a kind thing to say, and appreciated by any down to earth, self-respecting woman. Yet these words become less effective in an effort to spark a romantic connection and stand out from all the other guys who tell her the same exact thing.

Keeping this in mind, could see how upon initially meeting this new girl, I may have already distinguished myself from 95% of the other guys by simply talking about something other than her looks, in this case, Costa Rica?

My experience was, a great deal of "first date" pressure lifted, and she went and spoke with great excitement about her own traveling adventures. While we are not currently married with kids, it was a fun first date and there were more that followed it.

This principle can be applied in almost any situation and have a positive effect. The person interviewing you is human, and has passions and interests of their own. An exception to this may be if you're applying for a job with a robot (I have yet to have met anyone who has experienced this, and even then, it would probably be fun to ask the robot about their interests). I'm sure people ask Siri all the time.

PLAN OF ATTACK:
Now that you've done your research and are feeling confident, what else can you do to prepare for this big meeting? I would recommend getting a few books that specifically focus on the interview portion of a job search (questions commonly asked, proper responses), or talk to that new employer friend of yours about questions they ask and what great responses they have heard over the years. *The essential guide for hiring and getting hired* by Lou Adler is a great book with lots of solid information, written by a highly experienced person on the subject of running companies and hiring people . Much of the content in the book are tools, information, and strategies for the *employer* to use in selecting great employees. By reading this, it inevitably provides great insight to the job seeker (you). This book is very affordable and could be purchased on Amazon.

In almost any interview I have ever been on, they ask questions such as:

"What would you say are your biggest strengths and weaknesses?"

"Can you tell me about a very difficult situation you experienced at a previous job? How did you handle it and what was the outcome?"

"Why do you want to work for this company?"

With many of the questions they ask you, try to be specific and how it could be applicable to the position you are applying for. An example would be the question above about the "Share a difficult situation experienced how it was handled, and the outcome." If you are applying for a job as a personal trainer and you have previous experience working as a trainer, do your best to use an example from the same field when answering. It will demonstrate an ability to perform the specific job you are applying for to the interviewer. If you can't think of anything specific to the same job, or you're venturing into a new field, just do your best to give any specific example from your previous work history.

Even if you're applying for your first job or have minimal work experience, be creative and ask if you can give the interviewer a hypothetical answer. In any of these examples, the interviewer has some idea where you are at in the process, so don't stress out! I have been stumped by many questions over the years, and learned that you don't have to rush your answer. Take your time and ask them if you can have a few moments to think about it. I've never heard someone say "no" to me when I asked them for a little extra time to give them a relevant answer. In fact, an employer friend of mine told me that he noticed that those who responded very quickly to tough, open ended questions had more of a tendency to lie. Skilled interviewers tend to ask different types of questions that force the person interviewing away from giving answers on auto pilot. A good interviewer wants a candidate to really think about their response. It's better to answer a question appropriately and effectively, than to rush and say something out of context or foolish.

One of the BEST situations is when you have a friend that works at the company you are interviewing with. This has happened to me on different occasions, and my friend tells me almost exactly what the person will be asking me and what types of answers they are looking for. NICE!

As it also relates to figuring out different types of questions asked during an interview, Paul Powers discussed a certain idea in his book: *Winning the Job Interview.* To summarize, Powers wrote that whether you are aware of it or not, you already know many questions almost any interviewer will ask you.

Now, you might be thinking, "I do?"

"Yes," Powers suggested, because lots of questions will be asked based on YOUR resume. This is why it is of great importance to know the information on it inside and out. He wrote: "Take each item on your resume-that's every item- and justify why it's there. It should say something great about you. If it's boring, edit it out. If it highlights one of your strengths, it's in." The author goes on to encourage the job seeker (you) to come up with "interesting and engaging stories that highlight all the wonderful things you can bring to a new employer." The benefits of doing this in preparation for an interview can clearly speak for themselves. Consequently, you will feel more confident and enthusiastic going into the interview, which are traits any employer values in a potential job candidate.

I have also found that "role-playing" some potential interview questions with a friend or family member before your interview significantly reduced any anxiety I was having, and made me feel much more self-assured going into the interview. It would also help you to practice asking the questions that YOU plan on asking in a role playing. This way not only can this person you role play with have an opportunity to provide feedback on the types of questions you ask, but the act of hearing the question aloud can provide you feedback unto itself. Better to regret a question you asked in a role play than on an actual interview!

IT WORKS.

INTERVIEWING THE INTERVIEWER:

Here's the tricky part. *What questions will you ask the person(s) conducting the interview?* I actually learned about the power of "role reversal" when I went on some interviews a few years ago for jobs that had nothing to do with my interests. Just for the fun of it, I began "interviewing the interviewer." Lo and behold, the ENERGY IN THE ROOM SHIFTED, and before I knew it, the employer seemed set on convincing me about why their company was superior to others in the field. My suggestion when it comes to this would be to take a few job interviews that you have NO interest in to practice this principle just for fun, (because looking for work is fun, obviously).

I will elaborate more on different types of interview questions in the next chapter.

An important tool I learned through trial and error is to not only write down the questions I want to ask on an interview, but to bring a notepad containing these written questions with me into the interview. I cannot tell you how many times I had many good questions I planned to ask, but forgot to do so during the interview either because I was sidetracked by the interviewer's questions, came up with new questions of my own, got nervous, etc. This was especially true with questions I had learned or read about to ask in an interview and wanted to test out in a real setting. Since it was new to me, I would completely forget those questions, and would remember only AFTER the interview was over.

Some of the questions you plan to ask may get answered before you ask them, or you may even decide during the interview that the question you had in mind was irrelevant. The idea here is that if interviewer(s) have a notepad with questions they plan to ask and notes to take, why shouldn't you?! This is YOUR interview to be prepared for by taking the necessary steps to ensure you shine!

PLAYING THE FIELD:

Have you ever noticed that girls or guys (depending on your sexual preference) seem to be *more attracted to you when you're in a committed relationship, or are dating other people at the time of interaction?*

Well, *this same concept applies on an interview.* We humans are attracted to a challenge. The following question provides a practical example of this philosophy.

Q: What candidate do you suppose would portray an attitude of confidence and self-respect more?

Guy #1) The guy who DESPERATELY wants this ONE job, and therefore is probably extremely anxious and overeager in their interactions with an employer, or

Guy #2) The guy who goes into the interview and knows what he REALLY wants, and also has the inner confidence knowing that he has TWO OTHER JOB OPPORTUNITIES in the next week that he would be perfectly content with.

Having different job interviews lined up simultaneously not only logically increases your odds of getting hired somewhere, but also alleviates some of the pressure you would have going into the interview. Additionally I have found that going on job interviews when I currently have a job creates a similar effect.

In dating, the same principle can apply. I have noticed that in times when I initially meet a girl and go on the first few dates, my frame of mind is noticeably more casual if I'm currently talking to other girls as well. There is less of a "she's the one, I better not screw this up" mentality, and more of a "there are plenty of fish in the sea" mindset.

The basic idea here......... is that there is POWER IN CHOICE, SO USE IT!

KEY POINTS TO REMEMBER FROM CHAPTER 4:

- Become an expert on both the company and the person interviewing you. Find out about what the person's interests, passions, and hobbies are before the interview. (whenever possible)

- Establishing a good rapport from the start with a genuine interest in the other person. It will help ease initial interview anxiety and get the other person to like you.

- Read some other books on job interviews; learn common interview questions and be ready to give a proper response. Practice by role playing the interview with friends and family.

- Practice the art of interviewing the interviewer with legitimate and well thought out questions. Try to schedule 2-3 job interviews within the same few weeks to increase your odds of being hired while alleviating the pressure of putting all your eggs in one basket.

CHAPTER 5: THE BIG DATE

By now you have put in the time and effort to pick a career, apply for jobs, network, set up a date/time for the interview, and prepare accordingly. Congratulations! You've made it this far, so be proud of yourself.

Ok, ………now what?

I'm glad you asked.

As I mentioned before, I've spent a lot more time on job hunting and interviews than I planned to, or wanted to, for that matter.

IT'S A FORM OF ART:

Everything: from the way you walk, communicate, make eye contact, smile, and carry yourself during the interview is a form of art. It takes grace, focus, practice, discernment, and perseverance.

One way I like to look at a job interview is as a conversation. Every person differs with their level of conversational skills, but the main objective is to determine if the position is a good fit for both parties involved. Too many people make the mistake of thinking the interview is one sided, where the person(s) interviewing you have all the power and control. I certainly used to think this way, but then I realized it wasn't true. By turning an interview into a two sided conversation, I believe that the objective will become much clearer for everyone, and be a reminder that you are in control of making the decision if the position is one you really want.

Referring back to the book *"Winning the Job Interview,"* Paul Powers does an excellent job of summing up different types of communication people use. Passive, Assertive, and Aggressive are the three categories Powers elaborates on in a portion of the book. He states that most people use passive and aggressive communication, but the goal is to be *assertive* in communicating when going in for a job interview. I strongly recommend that you learn the distinction between these types of communicating, and work on being more assertive in your communication with others. If you have friends or former employers you respect and feel comfortable around, it would be beneficial to ask them what type of way you communicate(d) with them in most interactions. It may initially sting a bit to hear their feedback, but at least this way you will know where you can improve. The truth is, we are often unaware of the way we come across to others. Many times our intentions are good, but we can come across in a somewhat negative way simply by using a certain voice tone or not making a conscious effort to communicate clearly.

Dr. Powers also mentioned how a person can check with a local community college and find some courses that address these communication styles. Sometimes companies will have programs that offer teaching tools as well. You can usually check with the Human Resources department regarding these types of programs.

The way you communicate with others is of monumental importance, so it would pay off to put in the extra effort in this area. Remember that emailing, texting, etc. are also forms of communication, and in many instances people write in a similar style to the way they speak. Even in an instance when the job field you work in doesn't involve as much social interaction, you will still need to speak with the employer before you get hired. Moreover, if this didn't already cross your mind, enhancing your communication skills will help in your personal life as well!

CONTRIBUTE, BUT BE SELECTIVE:
In order to apply this principle, I first look at the company, and think of what I CAN ADD. I will also think of the unique gifts I have, along with positive attributes and skills former employers, friends, and family has told me in the past. In one of his books, real estate tycoon Donald Trump wrote that if he could summarize the three most important attributes he looks for in an employee, it would be "loyal, responsible, and professional." This being said, it certainly wouldn't hurt to develop a few of these traits in addition to the ones you already feel you possess. I then consider RELEVANT, SPECIFIC questions and points I need to ask or make throughout my interactions with the employer. All these steps listed are taken in an effort to deliver a message. The message is that I'm a highly competent, responsible, and talented prospect for the job, and THEY (the company) would be lucky to have ME.

An example I could use in regards to asking specific questions during an interview was for a County Job I interviewed for last year in San Diego. I was being interviewed by two different people at once, and they were asking me a lot of challenging questions. When it came time for me to ask some of my own, I already had several in mind. One question I asked was about how high of a turnover rate there was in their company. Again, since I became a somewhat experienced job hunter, I knew that in my field the reason these companies had these high turnover rates was usually because they were not good places to work, more or less.

I specified that I wanted stability in my job, and wasn't looking for a 'transitional job.' I also stated that working at a place where there was consistency within the staff was important to me. Upon asking this, one of the women interviewing me immediately exclaimed, "That was a GREAT question! And your reason for asking it was even better!"

This was the first time I remember someone actually getting excited over a QUESTION I asked in an interview. Ironically, I wasn't trying to impress them AT ALL with that question. I was asking simply because the places I worked at before had a VERY HIGH turnover, and there were good reasons why. Learning from these experiences made me take a closer look at future companies I was applying to. Although this was a job I didn't get offered, it certainly taught me a lot and provided me with more network contacts that I'm still currently in communication with.

FIGURING OUT IF THE COMPANY IS A GOOD PLACE TO WORK

A few more examples of questions I have asked during an interview, or general types of questions one can ask to assess the quality of a business are:

- Of your twenty employees, what percentage work full time and have a full case load?
- How does this BMW location compare in its quarterly sales to the other BMW dealerships in the region?
- How large is the volume of customers that your company works with in comparison to similar companies in the local area?
- Of your employees currently working here, what is the average length of time they have been employed with your company?

These questions are specifically targeted to sift the remaining successful companies from the ones that are struggling. So many people I have talked to in the last few years got laid off because of their company downsizing. Think of how many industries have a few companies that are monopolizing, while the other ones are already out of business, or headed down that path.

I am by no means affirming that just because a company is struggling financially means they are 'bad,' and one should not take a job working for them. At the very least, it could be a great resume builder and lead to other things for you. I am sharing these things because I think it is important now more than ever to be a 'smart shopper' when it comes to looking for work. Having these jobs where the company is in financial turmoil and has a lack of stability in their workforce taught me the hard way to become more assertive in the selection process.

http://www.glassdoor.com is a helpful website that offers feedback on different companies to work for. A lot of the comments include information on if the company is a "scam" or not, and other details about the quality of working there. Reviewers list pros and cons of the company, and rate the company overall. I personally looked up various companies I have worked for over the years, and many of the reviews seemed to be fair and accurate. Additionally the website is also a search engine for jobs being offered. It is a very nice luxury to be able to look at the quality and reviews of places you are applying for all on the same website. Throughout my experience going on job interviews, my observation has been that the companies which I later found out negative things about seemed to get defensive or anxious when asked specific questions about their company. In contrast, when I would ask the SAME EXACT questions to a company I had heard positive things about, they seemed to be happy to answer these questions and would provide me with as much relevant information as I needed to know. Again, the goal here is not to get the person(s) interviewing you upset, but to be discerning; asking relevant questions that provide you with answers you need to know in order to make a wise, well-informed decision later on.

If you are being courteous and innocuous yet demonstrating a certain level of preparedness and assertiveness in the questions you ask, it is very possible that the reason these employers may appear frustrated is simply because their company is not doing well. Legitimate, well thought out questions can be bringing this to the surface. Remember, these people are human too, and it's very unfortunate if their company is struggling. I am always saddened to hear of so many places recently going out of business and see restaurants or other establishments vacant that had been around for years.

Still, please don't hop onboard a sinking ship and go down with them! If you sense a pattern in people interviewing you getting defensive at questions you ask, maybe you're picking a lot of the struggling companies and need to improve your research beforehand. This is a possibility, as there are usually (and unfortunately) more openings with the companies that have poor reputations or just financially struggling nowadays. Or, you are more than likely crossing the fine line of being aggressive and insulting, as opposed to assertive and curious.

If this is the case, continue to work on this skill. Practice more role plays with friends or family members; record your interview questions on a tape recorder, etc. Continue to do things previously mentioned so that you have confidence in an interview that you've done the best you could. The goal should always be to make an effort to improve on each area of your job interview skills. With some skills you may improve quickly and not have many issues, while others may take a little longer and require more work. See each part of the process as a learning experience, rather than getting down on yourself if something doesn't work out the way you thought it would.

DEMONSTRATING VALUE :

I will share with you how I got my most recent job. I already had a contact that referred me over, which was obviously a good thing. When I initially spoke with the Executive Director, I mentioned the referral, and how they had said good things about the company. I stated, "I trust so and so, and since she had good things to say about your company, I'd like to know more." I personally LOVE using this line. Not only is it establishing a common connection between you and the employer, but I've noticed that the person will then make a conscious effort in making a good impression. This is usually an attempt (sometimes unconscious) to be in congruence with the impression your connection had of them.

I hope you can also see how this statement is different from that of a person who is acting desperate for work, i.e. unworthy, and indirectly communicates this to a potential employer. No bueno!

I made sure to subtly communicate from the start that I have HIGH STANDARDS for myself and where I'd like to work.

Next, I researched the company and see how I could make the biggest contribution and make myself an asset instantly in the employer's eyes.

> **Positive #1:** My line of work is female dominant, so being male can be a positive thing. I checked the staff roster to see if there was a shortage of males, which there was.
>
> **Positive #2:** I am both aware and experienced in the specific populations I want to work with; one of these being school based adolescent work. On their website, I noticed they had a contract with a charter school, which I made a note to ask about during the interview.
>
> **Positive #3:** I like doing group therapy, so I looked on the site for their current groups, and then I thought of groups that I could add to that list.

During the interview, I casually mentioned that I had been offered a few similar type positions recently, (which was true) but I wanted to know what separated their company from these other ones. The director mentioned some good points, and began to

QUALIFY the company to me, not vice versa. After hearing that the company had just contracted with one school and was looking to expand, I was able to let her know that I was really passionate about working in schools and would love to help network in this area. Additionally I mentioned that I had relevant job experience working with kids of all ages, so I could be flexible to best meet the company's needs. I made a few other points, along with positive observations I had made about her company. I gave specific examples of ways that I felt I could best contribute, and used relevant work experience as it would pertain to the job description. I asked her if she felt the things I had mentioned would be useful and lucrative for her company, to which she agreed.

Needless to say, I was offered the position on the spot. Of course this isn't ALWAYS the case, and there have been interviews I thought went terrific, only to not get the job. The point is, with anything, it takes persistence and practice to enhance one's skills in something, this being the job seeking process. I've by no means mastered it, and have a lot to learn. Yet over time, I've learned what works, what doesn't work, and have gradually developed this skill.

Just for fun, let's pretend I went on a date with the gorgeous Beyonce with the same kind of mindset. After knowing only a little of what she's like, I tell her that based on what my friend told me, she seems interesting and I'd like to know more about her.

Upon meeting, I'm not going to act like an over eager obsessed fan and ask for an autograph on the dinner napkin of the restaurant we are eating at. Instead, I casually ask her what she thinks makes her different and interesting from the other beautiful celebrities in Hollywood. This probably wouldn't be the very first thing I would say, but I'd be sure to mention a type of question like this.

The idea here is that by asking questions like this in a confident, nonchalant way, I would INSTANTLY communicate to her that I not only value myself, but am looking past her beauty and fame and I'm indirectly saying: THOSE THINGS AREN'T ENOUGH FOR ME. The irony is: it's actually true. I love beautiful women as much as the next guy, but I'm also selective when it comes to a potential long term partner. In the same way I feel confident about my ability to be successful in my line of work and feel like I deserve the best, I have also dated some rather attractive women, and feel comfortable enough to challenge one to demonstrate some value to me aside from her looks.

Assuming she began to answer the question, I begin listening to her and what she's saying, and from there discern what kind of woman she is. I might even tease her a bit just for fun during this period.

To summarize, even if throughout the date we both realized it wasn't a good fit, (only because she reminded me that she was married to Jay-Z) I'm sure she would have appreciated and perhaps even impressed that I was interested in things about her that 90 % of the people she generally meets don't even bother to ask. Maybe she wasn't attracted to me, but it could be possible that she became 'crazy in love' again.

KEY POINTS TO REMEMBER FROM CHAPTER 5:

- Just like in dating, having options and knowing your worth can alleviate anxiety and lessen the pressure of putting all your hope into one job opportunity (or a romantic interest).

- Learn the art of making a job interview into more of a conversation. Remember to value yourself and determine what you can contribute.

- Come up with specific, relevant questions to ask in order to find out if the job is a good fit for you. Doing so will demonstrate assertiveness and the employer will want to qualify the company to you and not the other way around.

- Continue to think of qualities, skills, and experience that would directly benefit the hiring company, and mention them throughout the interview as is necessary.

CHAPTER 6: WRAPPING UP THE INTERVIEW & THE AFTERMATH

Hopefully your interview is going well after all we've talked about, and you have a renewed zeal and confident approach to your job hunt. Now that you've established your credibility and have decided that the potential employer is someone/somewhere you would like to work, how do you wrap things up? My most recent position that was offered to me on the spot was, in my experience, the exception to the rule. Assuming this isn't the case, there are a few different approaches I've come across or found to be effective.

AGREE TO AGREE:

In *How to win friends and influence people,* the author Dale Carnegie talks about the power of getting the other person to say "Yes." I've also learned about this concept in sales as well. To be honest, I felt at first that this approach sounded somewhat contrived and unauthentic, so I was reluctant to use it. However, I've FOUND it to be effective in a context when I've used tact, precision, and sincerity to get my point across.

An example of this could be demonstrated from my last interview. I could have asked the employer, "So, would my experience and willingness to focus on working in the school setting be one of the more important things that you are looking for in a job candidate?" To which she would most likely reply "Yes, it is very important." The truth is, not only is this very powerful way to clarify the benefit of me being hired, but it was a legitimate question that I wanted to know, and she might not have agreed to its importance. If that was the case, at least I now knew that this wasn't a major concern to her at the moment.

BREAK IT DOWN:
Next, I have a few choices. I can either:
1) Decide the job wasn't for me, or
2) Inquire more.

The first option could lead me to simply thank the person for their time, and politely say that the job wasn't going to be a good fit for me. That or I could go through with the rest of the interview, and kindly turn down the position if it was offered to me down the road.

If I wanted to inquire more, I could have then asked something along the lines of: *"What would you say are the most important qualities you are looking for in a job candidate right now?"* Her answer would provide me with a better idea of

A) What the company wanted.

B) What I could potentially contribute to the company.

Over the last year or so, I've used a combination of questions such as the example above, along with statements that aimed to communicate both my enthusiasm for the position and reasons why I could be a valuable asset. It is also helpful to know how far along they are in the hiring process, and when you may receive an answer by. Many times I went on interviews while I was currently working another job, so I needed some type of clarification of what to expect in terms of how soon they needed someone to start, length of training, etc., so I could give my current employer a fair notice before leaving. Not only will the interviewer respect that you are being considerate of your current boss, (many employees leave without notice) it's a way to "Act as if" you are getting hired. It demonstrates confidence and assertiveness, which are traits any employer in their right mind would want in a candidate. In a recent conversation I had with an established professional about my book, she mentioned the one question she had asked at the end of an interview was, "So when do you want me to get started?" She told me that it would sometimes be met with a comical or surprised reaction; yet she was hired in every interview she had concluded using that specific question.

CLOSE THE DEAL

I've recently read a few books about trying to close the job towards the end of an interview. Bob Firestone, who wrote *The Ultimate Guide to Job Interview Answers,* suggested saying something like this: "Do we seem to be in agreement that I have the qualifications, skills, and experience it will take to succeed here? (Assuming they say yes) Great! Would it be reasonable to expect a formal offer for the position by Thursday of next week? I want to ask you to put your faith in me and give me the job." I personally have less experience with this type of approach, but I mentioned it because I could see its benefit and wanted to give the reader (you) some different options to consider. Who doesn't love options?!

The "close" questions, "yes" questions, and "positive" statements mentioned above are just a few examples that can be used. I am a firm believer in taking the good, and leaving the rest. While some of these ideas may not seem comfortable to use at first, (as I once felt) I would recommend using the approach that would feel most natural to you. It may still feel a bit uncomfortable, but try it anyway. Maybe try it twice, just for practice. You can always go for a job interview somewhere you'd never actually work at simply to EXPERIENCE the reactions you may get from using the tools. There's a chance you may just be pleasantly surprised with the results. And let's be honest: if you're not working, you probably have a little extra time to go on a bunch of interviews and practice these things!

FINISH, AND FINISH STRONG:
   After the interview, assuming you didn't get hired on the spot, or fired on the spot (insert smile with wink) for asking too many great questions, YOU ARE STILL IN THE GAME. One can still demonstrate quality of character and keep a positive impression with the person that interviewed you (hoping there was one) by doing certain things.

   I have a friend who worked in a position where he had to interview people for several years, and he told me that he was most impressed by a certain candidate that sent him A CARD in the mail which thanked him for taking the time to interview him. I just recently heard this, and if I didn't already have a job, I would certainly try it!

   What I had begun to do before I got my last job was something I mentioned earlier in the book. I would send an email thanking the interviewer for his/her time, and that I looked forward to hearing from them. Being aware that these people probably interviewed A LOT of people, I would also maybe mention something very brief that we had connected with on a positive note. The goal was to be very casual and yet still aim to separate myself from other candidates and keep my name fresh in their mind.

   Throughout my interviews with different employers, several mentioned to me that it is beneficial to specify a follow up email with anything you felt needed clarification from your actual interview. For example, perhaps there was something you forgot to mention in the interview, and you felt that mentioning it in the email could really help your chances of being hired. Or, you may need to correct something that had been misstated or omitted during the interview.

Another thing I repeatedly heard was to write something in the email that expands or comments on a job related situation the employer may have asked you.

You may write something along these lines:

"In our meeting the other day you mentioned ......(the problem / issue) and the more thought about I wondered if we could try ......(the possible solution) "

In any of these cases, the follow up email is the time when you can address these types of things as you see fit.

I am no dating expert, but I'm sure a follow up email/text/phone call after a date would be a good thing to do if you wanted to see the person again. Even if there wasn't a shot in hell you had with them, I'm sure they would appreciate the gesture.

KEY POINTS TO REMEMBER FROM CHAPTER 6:

- Ask leading type questions that get the other person saying YES. This is a very effective way to confirm things that are agreed upon during the interview and can allow you to leave on a highly positive note (assuming they don't just decide to hire you on the spot!)

- Get specific details about what the employer wants in a job candidate. By the end of the interview you should be able to determine if the job is something you would want to move forward with.

- Finish strong by staying in contact with your employer after the interview by sending an email or a card. Doing so will keep you fresh in their mind during the decision process.

IN SHORT:

Reading up to this point, you should have a few new ideas that you can use on your journey. If you already knew and applied everything mentioned throughout the content of this book, you are much more ahead of the game than I was. Hopefully there were some good reminders. Thank you for humoring me and continuing to read anyway!

This book is meant to be a reference tool, not a novel. It is a lot easier to read the book once, say "Ok, I got it," and then get frustrated right away if you don't hear back about job inquiries, get nervous during an interview, get turned down from a job you had wanted, and subsequently feel like it hasn't worked. The likelihood will be to continue this as a practice, and keep referring back to the book when challenges present themselves. It has certainly taken me a long time to work on these things, as shown by the fact that I've written a book on the subject! These are skills I continue to work on myself. As with most skills, things don't necessarily change overnight, so don't get discouraged when you experience this. It will most likely be a process of being persistent and learning how to develop and improve your skills in this area. Experience is quite a fantastic teacher if you listen to her lessons.

More importantly, I hope that this book will encourage and challenge you to take some time and think about what your strengths are as a person, and how this can be applied for finding a job that you really desire. It is challenging to maintain a level of self-confidence and go after what you're passionate about, especially if you keep getting told that places aren't hiring for work, or not hearing back for months at a time about a job you actually want. I hope you believe me when I tell you that I can certainly relate to feeling this way. Having the support from family, friends, or acquaintances having similar struggles during this process can be very helpful. I would also strongly suggest that you seek out a few people who you know had been looking for work and found a job, and ask them how they did it.

Deepak Chopra, is an amazingly inspiring writer and has written tons of books that are sold around the world. In one of his books I read, *THE SEVEN SPIRITUAL LAWS OF SUCCESS*, he speaks about the "Law of Dharma." Simply yet eloquently put, he wrote:

"The Law of Dharma says that we have taken manifestation in physical form to fulfill a purpose. According to this law, you have a unique talent and a unique way of expressing it. There is something you can do better than anyone else in the whole world. And for every unique talent and unique expression of that talent, there are also unique needs."

Additionally, the more you realize your potential, while remaining focused on your individual gifts and the best way to use these gifts; you will strengthen the belief in the positive impact you bring to any given situation. This is not only in regards to work, but in any area of life.

Convince yourself of what makes you great, and it will inevitably communicate that same message to others.

About the Author

Since enrolling in graduate school in 2009, I had spent an astonishing amount of time in the pursuit of work in my specific field. I continued to hear more stories from friends, family, and acquaintances that experienced the shame, anger, and lowered self-worth that comes with continued rejection and an inability to provide for oneself. The decision to write the book "The Job Inner-View" came to me as sort of an epiphany one morning in late 2012, as I wanted to write about all the different successful and creative methods I used to find work in hopes that it could help encourage and inspire millions of other unemployed Americans. Throughout the course of writing my book, I was able to interview various well known and highly experienced employers; gaining both insight and feedback on how one should go about finding work in today's economy, as well as recurring similarities in success stories from employees I interviewed who found work.

A major concern that seems to go unaddressed with job searching today has to do with the exceptionally fast degree to which technology has advanced, which I believe BOTH employers/employees alike are struggling to catch up with for various reasons. Many companies now use computers to sort through specific keywords to sift through the thousands of resumes they receive a week. Typical job seekers spend hours filling out application after application and will hardly hear back from a human being in order to establish a quality connection, which research shows is essentially why people are hired for jobs. My mission has been to create an innovative way for both employees/employers to connect more quickly and proficiently. One of several methods I currently use to carry this out is my blog site and

Facebook page: https://www.facebook.com/TheJobInnerview where I share success stories of newly hired individuals, as well as postings from both jobs offered/needed from mutual contacts and friends of mine to help bring people together through social networking. I also began contacting Universities and spoke to graduate students in helping prepare them with tools for finding work upon graduating.

~ Scott Engler

Author of "The Job Inner-View"

"When we give from a place of love, rather than a place of expectation, more usually comes back to us than we could have ever imagined." ~ Susan Jeffers

Read more at www.thejobinnerview.com.

Made in the USA
Lexington, KY
20 January 2017